Left-Handed Needlepoint

REGINA HURLBURT

DRAWINGS BY ROBIN HALL

VAN NOSTRAND REINHOLD COMPANY
NEW YORK   CINCINNATI   TORONTO   LONDON   MELBOURNE

For Susan, who is left-handed, and
Allen, who made it all happen.

Van Nostrand Reinhold Company Regional Offices:
New York   Cincinnati   Chicago   Millbrae   Dallas
Van Nostrand Reinhold Company International Offices:
London   Toronto   Melbourne

Library of Congress Catalog Card Number: 70-39806
ISBN 0 442 23596 8 cl.
ISBN 0 442 23597 6 pb.

Designed by Allen Hurlburt
Printed in England

Published in 1972 by Van Nostrand Reinhold Company,
a Division of Litton Educational Publishing, Inc.
450 West 33rd Street, New York, N.Y. 10001
and by Van Nostrand Reinhold Company Limited,
25-28 Buckingham Gate, London S.W. 1

Published simultaneously in Canada by
Van Nostrand Reinhold Ltd.
16 15 14 13 12 11 10 9 8 7 6 5 4 3 2 1

Contents

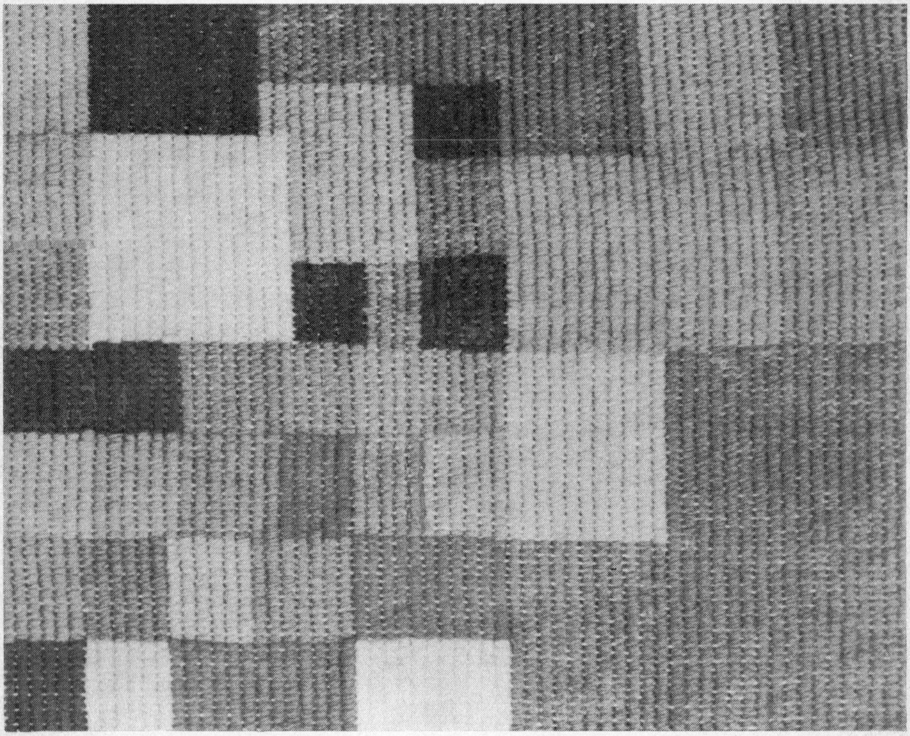

Foreword

SO YOU'RE LEFT-HANDED? Right! So am I! It has been said that over the centuries one hundred to two hundred million people started life out left-handed. For centuries it was considered an ill omen. In fact, the word "sinistral," or left-handed, comes from the Latin *sinistrum*, which means "evil," "unlucky," "inauspicious," and from which we derive the word sinister. Da Vinci and Charlemagne are just two of many in the history of the human race who were left-handed, and I would not consider them unlucky.

In a sense, left-handed people *are* unlucky; so many of us have had to struggle for years with the simple daily tools of living which have always been designed for the right-handed. I have searched in vain for a double-serrated knife for sectioning oranges and grapefruit, and only in recent years have left-handed scissors been manufactured.

A favorite hobby of mine is needlework; I enjoy any kind. It is a relaxing pastime and if the piece is small enough you can take it with you wherever you go. However, often to my dismay, it has been a slow process of self-teaching, since most instructors and books are for right-handed people. When I sought aid from one of the best needlework shops in the country, their personnel just shrugged and told me to hold my book up to a mirror. Such a maneuver is time-consuming and just leads to additional frustration. Most children would find this process dampening to any initiative or enthusiasm with which they originally approached the activity.

This little book came into being one afternoon, two summers ago. My daughter, who is also left-handed, commented to a left-handed friend that she felt fortunate that her mother was left-handed, in answer to our friend's remark that she had never been able to teach her daughters needlework because they were right-handed. I realized then that perhaps my own experiences with teaching myself the stitches for needlepoint could benefit others.

Needlecraft shops can give you much information about canvas and the wool needed for different-sized meshes, and they will also help you to work out your designs and color schemes. This book has as its modest aim to help you enjoy the working of your stitches.

Left-Handed Needlepoint

Canvas   IN THIS BOOK I will discuss the stitches that can be done on canvas and which come under the general category of needlepoint. First about the canvas — it is a mesh fabric that is woven of vertical and horizontal threads that are evenly spaced. The two basic canvases available are mono, which has single threads going in both directions to form the mesh, and penelope canvas, woven with double threads.

Warp (vertical) and woof (horizontal) threads of the mono canvas are equidistant from each other, and this material is usually available in white cotton. The number of mesh refers to the number of openings between the threads per inch. With mono canvas it can be as fine as 20 to 40 mesh to the inch and then the material is called gauze. Gauze is used for fine silk petit point.

The most popular mono canvases are 10, 12, or 14 mesh to the inch. They work easily and quickly and with the exception of two stitches — Half-Cross Stitch and the Rep Stitch — can be used for most designs.

Eight-mesh canvas is also quick and easy, but be sure your design lends itself to such a large stitch. It is most often used for small rugs.

In the penelope canvas or the double-mesh canvas, which has two threads in both the warp and the woof, the warp threads are closer together than the woof threads. Penelope canvas has greater versatility than the mono canvas. For example, a 9-18 penelope canvas (9 double threads per inch) may be used to combine fine detailing in your design with a fast-working background. Just separate the warp and woof threads in a specific area, and you will then have a single 18-to-the-inch mesh for the detailing. Be sure to use the thinner strand of wool for the fine work.

Always purchase the best quality canvas available; check it

Mono Canvas   *Penelope Canvas*

carefully to be sure that there are no flaws. It would truly be a waste of your time and effort to use materials that will not be long-lasting. When purchasing your canvas, keep in mind that you must plan a two-inch margin around your finished needlepoint.

The simplest and most easily applied material for binding your cut canvas is one-inch-wide masking tape, and when you have completed your canvas it is also just as easy to pull off. Keep in mind that the selvage edge of the canvas should be on the side.

Wool

The most popular and expensive material you can use for fine petit point — that is, work on a mesh requiring at least sixteen stitches per inch — is Filoselle silk. It is two-ply with each strand having six threads. You can use as many strands as the fine canvas or gauze will hold. On the other hand, you can also separate a strand of this silk and then combine it with a fine strand of wool for the highlighting of details.

The most versatile wool for needlepoint is Persian wool. It is two-ply, and comes in three-thread strands. You can separate the threads and use only one strand for petit point on a 10- or 12-mesh penelope canvas with the mesh separated, or you can use all three strands for the double mesh. Persian wool can be purchased in small quantities, sometimes even by the single strand for a tiny detail in your design.

Crewel wool will also make a fine petit point stitch. It is strong and comes in a very wide range of colors. A single, two-ply thread of crewel wool is perfect for petit point. You can multiply as many strands of crewel wool as your mesh opening will hold — sometimes as many as twelve strands can be used with a large rug mesh. The multiple strands of wool create a need to keep a careful tension control on all your stitches.

Tapestry wool is four-ply and comes in larger skeins than Persian wool. It can be used on 10-, 12-, and 14-mesh mono canvas or it can be separated into two-ply for petit point on a single mesh of a 10-mesh penelope canvas.

Rug wool is three-ply and is a rougher texture than the wools listed above. However, some of the finer, soft-textured wools have been used with 10-mesh canvas for Bargello designs. You will note further in this book a Bargello design that was worked with rug wool on 10-mesh canvas. It has the advantages of working quickly and showing results easily to encourage the beginner.

Needles

Originally in the early history of tapestry and needlepoint, needles were made of bone. It was not until the Sixteenth Century that the first iron needle appeared, and the steel needle of today has a versatility that our ancestors would envy.

Since needlepoint is today's version of tapestry weaving, your needlepoint needles are more apt to be marked tapestry needles and are available in packages of assorted sizes as well as being sold individually. They are made with a blunt point in order to prevent catching hold of the thread of the canvas. It is important that you use the correct size needle, so that it will pass smoothly through the mesh and not disturb the smoothness of the canvas. The size of the eye is proportioned to the needle's size and thickness. The higher the number of the needle, the finer the canvas and thread it is to be used with. For example, a #24 needle is used with silk thread on fine gauze petit point.

The most popular size needle is #17. It may be used with any of the 10- to 14-mesh-to-the-inch canvases and with both Persian and tapestry wool.

Rug needlepoint uses a #15 needle with tapestry or light rug wool. A #15 needle with light rug wool was used for the Bargello Stitch shown in a later chapter of this book.

How to Start Your Needlepoint

You will find that the stitch instructions in this book are the reverse of the usual right-handed instructions, and in some instances I have even changed the starting point, such as with the Basketweave Stitch, and the Long Cross Stitch with the overstitch. I feel that the ease you work with is as important as knowing how to work your stitches. Holding your canvas in a clumsy position, for example, takes away from the pleasure of doing needlepoint. Therefore, unless specifically noted, hold your canvas in the way that feels best to you. Always keep in mind a very important point: *All Your Stitches Should Go in the Same Direction* unless you wish to break the traditional pattern as I have shown in the Basketweave Stitch combined with the Continental Stitch. Another essential point: never secure your length of wool with a knot when you start, since this will leave a bump that may eventually show on your finished canvas. Instead, pull your wool through the first mesh from underneath, leaving about a half-inch length of wool. Hold this down flat with your index finger and begin your stitches, being sure to catch the bit of wool until it is completely worked into your stitches. Pull each subsequent length of new wool through the back of a half dozen completed stitches, and to finish it, do the same thing. Turn to the back of the canvas and run your needle through alternating stitches for about an inch and then clip the wool close to the canvas.

Some of your stitches can be completed in one stroke, whereas others will need the "into-the-canvas-and-then-up-from-beneath" method. It depends on the stitch as well as the stiffness of your canvas.

Another important thing to keep in mind is not to allow your wool to become "pulled," because after repeated pulling through the canvas, your yarn will be thinned out and not the fluffy wool you started with. The best way to avoid this is to keep your length of wool in the needle short — twelve to fifteen inches is enough. Also, the finer the wool, the shorter should be the length you use. Try to work evenly, without pulling your wool too tight

— since then your canvas will show — or leaving the wool loose, which will allow for accidental snagging.

Start working your canvas where the center of your design begins. Complete all of your design before beginning on the background.

The first seven stitches shown in this book are considered the basic stitches of needlepoint. If you become proficient in working with just these, you can be creative with design and texture. Then using the Tramé Stitch with any of these stitches, you will have the additional effect of a raised or "bump" texture in your work.

In time, as you become more experienced with needlepoint you will be curious to try other stitches shown in this book. They will widen your experience with different variations of texture. Some of the stitches like the Smyrna Cross Stitch or the Star Stitch will give you still another variation of the "bump" texture. Still others will lend themselves to a simple geometric design that can be your first in designing your own needlepoint canvas.

Ripping Your Mistakes

No matter how adept you are or how carefully you work, there can always be a mistake or a few stitches that do not look right. If you have enough respect for yourself and your work, you will feel that it is a shame to let them go uncorrected. Therefore, it is good to know how to rip them out. I believe that a sharp-pointed cuticle scissor is the best tool to use. The point curves slightly upward, and this is helpful in making sure that you do not catch your canvas when you are snipping the wool. Snip very carefully through the incorrect stitches, both on the above and the underneath sides. Next, with your fingers, pick the wool out. Now use a crochet needle or your tapestry needle to remove an additional two inches of wool. This should give you enough length of wool to thread into your needle, and you can proceed to finish it off on the underside of the canvas. Now use a fresh length of wool to redo the stitches you have ripped out on your canvas.

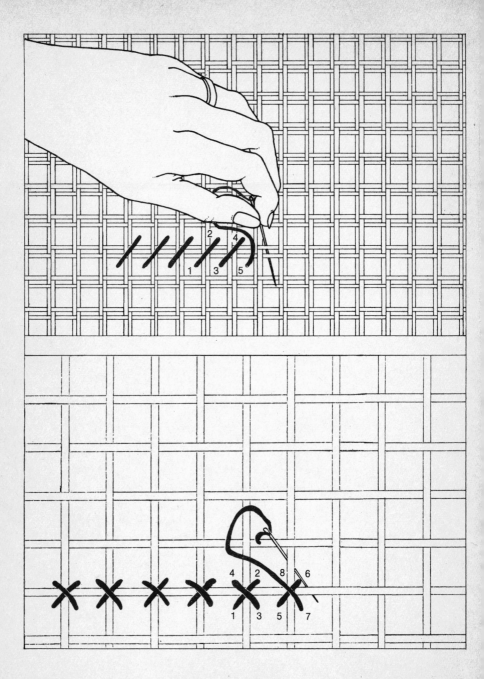

Half Cross Stitch

Half Cross Stitch

The Half Cross Stitch, which is short and slanted, is the simplest of the needlepoint stitches. However, it should only be done on penelope canvas, because the backing of the stitch is not strong enough to hold the mono canvas firm. The stitch needs the double threads of the penelope canvas to keep its shape.

Beginning at the most convenient point of your canvas and your design, stitch your first row, bringing your wool slantwise over the crossed threads of the canvas as shown in your illustration. When you have finished your first row, turn your canvas upside down and proceed to your second row; do this for each new row. As you work across your canvas your needle will go under the woof threads. For a change of design you can work from the top to the bottom of the canvas, and this will bring your needle under the warp threads of the canvas.

The Rep Stitch is another of the small slanted stitches, and bears a strong similarity to the Half Cross Stitch. It, too, can only be done on penelope canvas. It is stitched over each one of the horizontal canvas threads and crosses over the two vertical canvas threads in the same stitch.

Cross Stitch

Cross Stitch

This stitch, one of the oldest used in any kind of needlework, can be done on mono as well as penelope canvas. There are two ways to stitch the Cross Stitch. First, you can stitch a row of Half Cross Stitches; these will be the under stitches. Then turn your canvas around and reverse your stitch to form the second stroke. The second method is to complete each stitch in a single operation — under and over — as shown in the drawing. This method is recommended when working on mono canvas, as it keeps your canvas firm and your stitches neat.

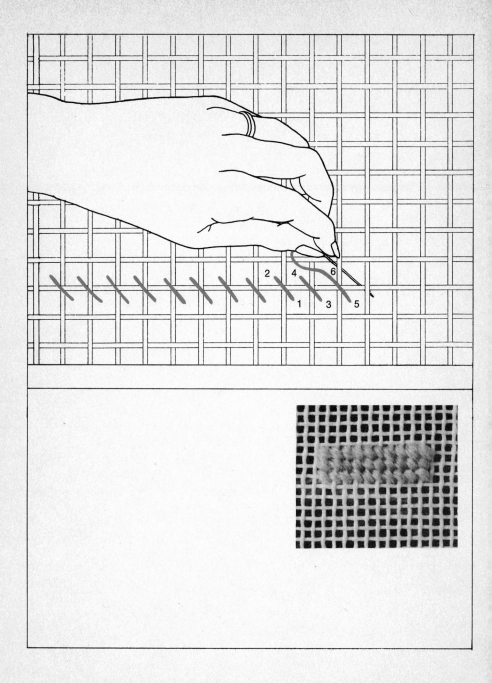

Continental or Tent Stitch

The Continental or Tent Stitch — another short, slanted stitch — is the most popular stitch for filling in your canvas around your design. It works easily for outlining shapes and filling in details of your design. It is used for petit point, and it works on either penelope or mono canvas. As with the Half Cross Stitch, you must keep turning your canvas upside down as you do each new row. The working of this stitch will pull your canvas out of shape, but that can be corrected in the blocking of your completed canvas. If you are planning to use your needlepoint for upholstery or a rug, I recommend the use of penelope canvas. The Continental Stitch used with penelope canvas will give you greater strength and wearability in your finished needlepoint.

Being left-handed, I have broken with the tradition that all slanted stitches must lean to the right. You will note that the stitches shown in the drawing slant to the left. Begin in the lower left-hand corner and bring your needle through at 1. Insert needle at 2, one mesh up and one mesh to the left. Bring needle through at 3, one mesh down and two meshes over. When you complete the row, turn your canvas upside down for the next row.

Your design may call for a combination of the Continental Stitch for your detailing and another stitch for filling the space around the detailing. Most times you will want to use the Basketweave Stitch for filling the large areas. Do not be deterred by the fact that your Continental Stitch will slant to the left while the Basketweave Stitch will slant to the right, as it always must. It will create an interesting pattern in your needlepoint. If you wish to give the traditional slant to your Continental Stitch, you must begin your first row of stitches in your design in the upside down position.

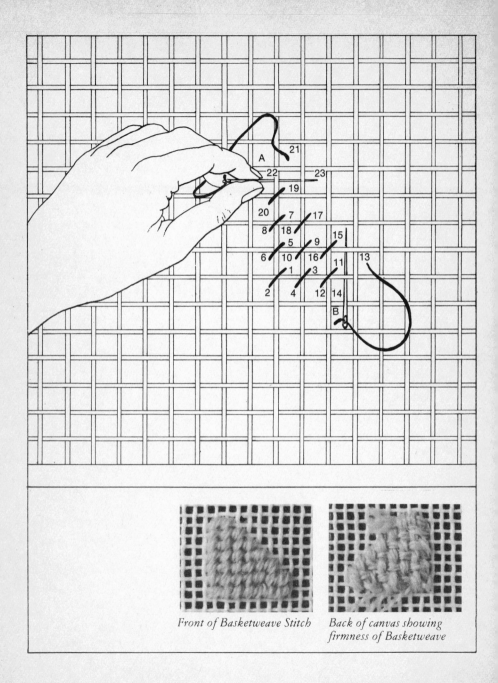

Front of Basketweave Stitch

Back of canvas showing firmness of Basketweave

Basketweave Stitch

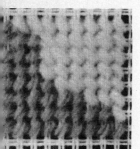

ontinental Stitch slanted the left combined with e Basketweave Stitch

The Basketweave Stitch, the best background-filler stitch, is more difficult to master than the Continental Stitch, but once you have done so, it will work quickly. It has several advantages: you can use it on either canvas, without having to keep turning the canvas for each row, and it will not pull your canvas out of shape; the weaving of the yarn on the underside of the canvas will give you greater strength and wearability.

For us, the left-handed, it truly must be a complete reversal of all right-handed instructions.

So here goes. Begin your stitches at the *lower left-hand corner.* The Basketweave Stitch begins like the Continental Stitch. Bring your needle up at 1 and down at 2 and slant your needle to come up at 3. Down at 4 and bring needle up vertically at 5. Down at 6 and up slanting at 7. Down at 8 and bring it up horizontally at 9. Down at 10 and again up horizontally at 11. Down at 12 and slanted up at 13. You will notice — and this is most important — that when you are working down the canvas your needle is always in a horizontal position (see A) parallel to the horizontal threads of the canvas. When you are working up the canvas, your needle is in a vertical position (see B). The only time your needle should be slanted is when you are preparing to begin a new row, such as from 5 to 6 and up to 7 for coming down the canvas, and from 11 to 12 and up at 13 for working up the canvas. With careful practice on a bit of canvas, your stitches will soon fall into a rhythm.

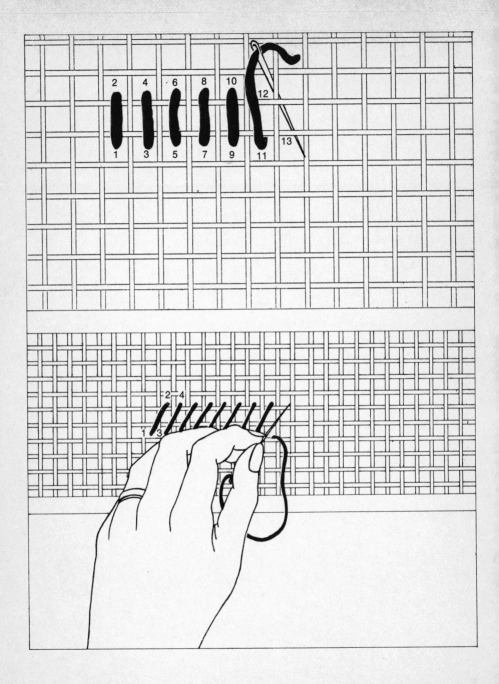

Straight Gobelin Stitch

Straight Gobelin

The Straight Gobelin Stitch, which derives its name from the tapestry produced at the Gobelin works in Paris, is basic and simple and works very quickly. You can make it cover as many as three or four meshes at a time, as long as you make sure your wool is full enough for your mesh size so that your canvas will not show through. I do not recommend that your stitch be any longer than four meshes since the wool may snag.

Start as many meshes down as you wish your stitch length to be — in this drawing three meshes long — bringing your needle through from underneath at 1 and holding your half inch of wool in place so that it will be caught into your stitches. Then insert your needle at 2 and bring it out one row over and as many meshes down at 3 as your stitch length will be. Continue to the end of the row, and turn your canvas upside down for the next row.

Slanting Gobelin Stitch

Slanting Gobelin

You begin the slanting Gobelin Stitch in the same way as the Straight Gobelin Stitch at 1. However, now you insert your needle one mesh over and as many meshes up as your stitch length will be at 2, then bring your needle through directly below. The position of your needle is vertical as it goes under the canvas threads from 2 to 3. Continue as shown in the drawing, and turn the canvas upside down for each new row.

Either of these stitches can be worked down-into-the-canvas-and-up-from-underneath or the stitch can be completed in one stroke as shown in the Straight Gobelin drawing.

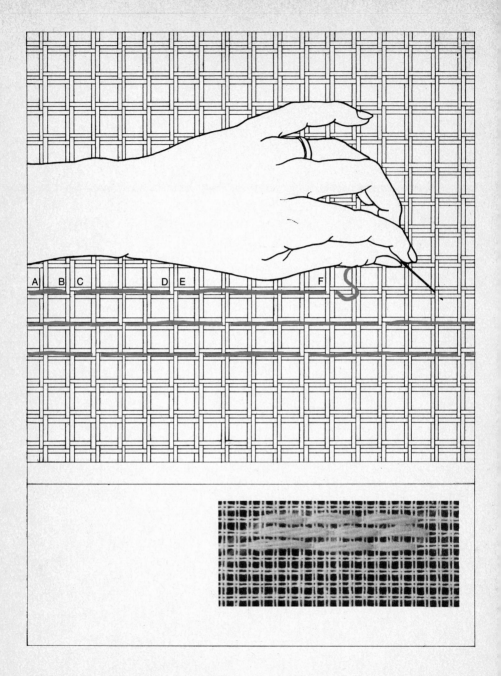

Tramé

Trame is an understitching that makes a nice padding for the Half Cross Stitch, the Cross Stitch, or the Gobelin Stitch. It can also be used for special details, such as initials of a signature or just to create a change of texture. Usually, the same color wool is used as in the overstitching, but you should split to half the usual strands for the Tramé. Sometimes, if it can be utilized in your design and for an interesting effect, use another color underneath, or Tramé in glossy silk of the same color as your wool. Whereas you split the yarn if you use wool, it may be necessary to use more than a single strand of silk.

Tramé stitches should be varied in length within each row, so that your overstitching won't form ridges. Tramé can be done either on mono canvas or penelope. If you do it on penelope canvas, stitch between your horizontal threads; on mono canvas, stitch through the horizontal threads. Bring the needle up through the canvas at A and go down into the canvas at B — up again at C, continuing thus to the end of the row. Complete all the Tramé stitching.

Refer to your numbered instructions for Half Cross Stitch, Cross Stitch, or Gobelin Stitch to complete your stitching.

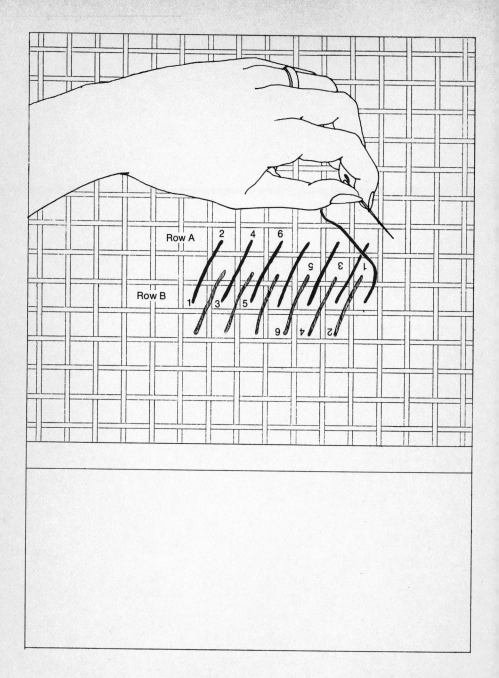

Interlocking Gobelin Stitch

The Interlocking — or as it is sometimes called, Encroaching — Gobelin Stitch is yet another variation of the Gobelin Stitch which works quickly and gives a good backing on the underside. As with the basic Gobelin, it can be as long as four meshes or as short as two meshes; just be sure your wool is heavy enough to cover all your meshes.

Bring your wool up from underneath the canvas at 1, go down into the canvas at 2, and continue as shown in the drawing until you finish your first row of stitches. Turn your canvas upside down and begin Row B, and when you have finished, repeat Row A.

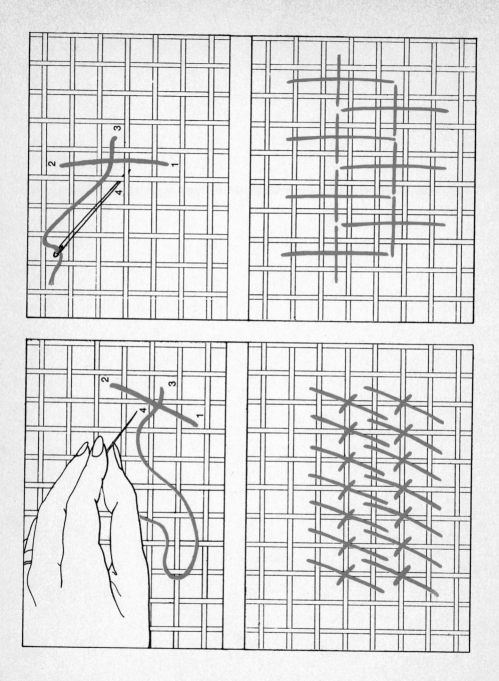

Long Gobelin with an Overstitch and Slanting Gobelin with an Overstitch

These two variations on the Gobelin Stitch are strong and make for an interesting texture. They may be used for small detailing or shallow background, such as creating the illusion of a picture frame around your needlepoint. Note the difference in stitch length between the straight and slanting stitch. The overstitch of the Slanting Gobelin is worked over a crossing of the warp and woof of the canvas as shown in the stitch marked 3 to 4. Keep your stitch length four meshes or under, as any longer stitch may snag.

The Long Gobelin with an overstitch should be five meshes long. Your overstitch will then cross over the third mesh and be three meshes long horizontally as in the drawing.

The left-handed stitcher may find it simpler to hold the canvas vertically and work from right to left across the canvas.

Long Gobelin with
an Overstitch

Slanting Gobelin with
an Overstitch

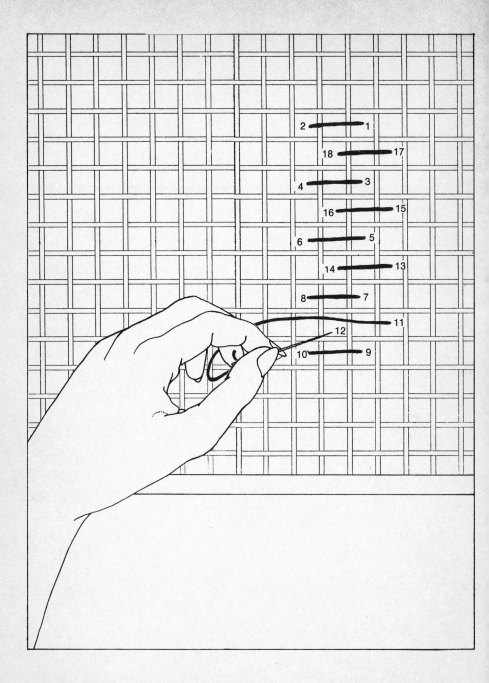

Brick Stitch

The Brick Stitch is still another variation of the Gobelin Stitch; it passes over an even number of threads of canvas, usually two to four. It is fast-working and a sturdy filler stitch; this method of working your stitches will give you a strong backing. If you check the back of your canvas after the first few rows, you will see the basketweave design it creates. As a left-handed stitcher you will probably find it more convenient to hold your canvas vertically. Start your first row, as shown, at 1; complete your stitch with putting your needle into the canvas at 2. Bring the needle up through the canvas at 3, having skipped a row of mesh. Continue until you have finished that row of stitches. Start your next row as shown with stitch 11 to 12 and continue filling in the rows of mesh that you have skipped in the working of your first row of stitches.

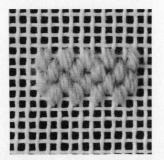

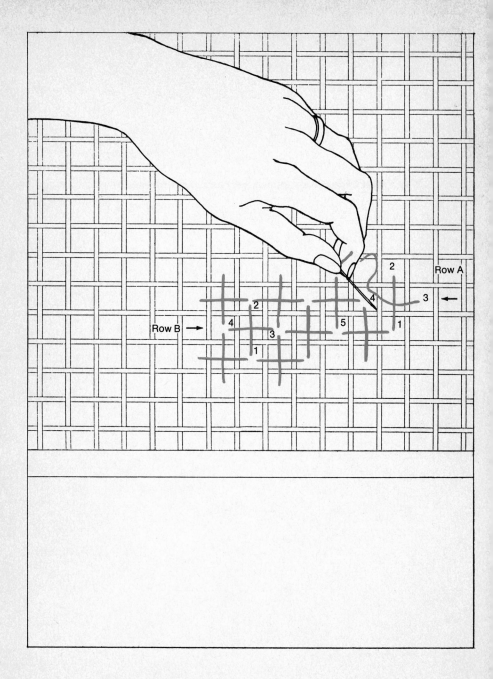

The Greek Cross Stitch

The Greek Cross Stitch, or the Upright Cross Stitch as it is sometimes called, can be worked on either the mono or penelope canvas, and is strong and snag-proof. You can use it as a background stitch or for detailing on a specific subject. As you will notice in the drawing, you must plan your stitches so that all the canvas is covered by your wool. Begin Row A on the right side of your canvas. Bring the needle up at 1, down into the canvas at 2, up again at 3, and down into the mesh at 4, coming up at 5, one mesh down and one mesh to the left.

Work Row B as shown in the drawing; it tucks under the horizontal bars of your Row A stitches. Always have your horizontal stitches over the vertical stitches.

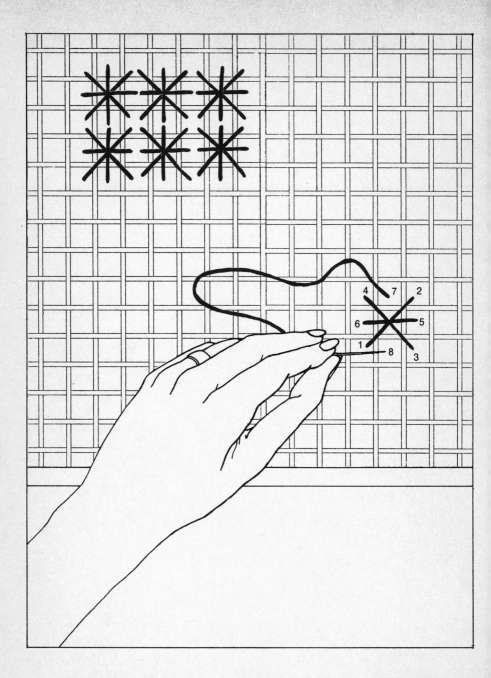

Smyrna Cross Stitch

The Smyrna Cross Stitch, which is basically made up of a regular Cross Stitch with an Upright Cross Stitch on top of it, can be worked on either mono or penelope canvas and gives a strong backing. As with the Greek Cross Stitch, you may use it to fill in the background of your design or for specific detailing within the design. Be prepared for the work to go slowly, since four strokes are needed to complete each stitch. Be sure that all your crosses are going in the same direction. Your final stitch should be in a vertical position: note 7 to 8. Your Upright Cross Stitch should always be your top stitch and if your design calls for a two-color Smyrna Cross Stitch, finish your regular Cross Stitch and then stitch your Upright Cross Stitch in your second color.

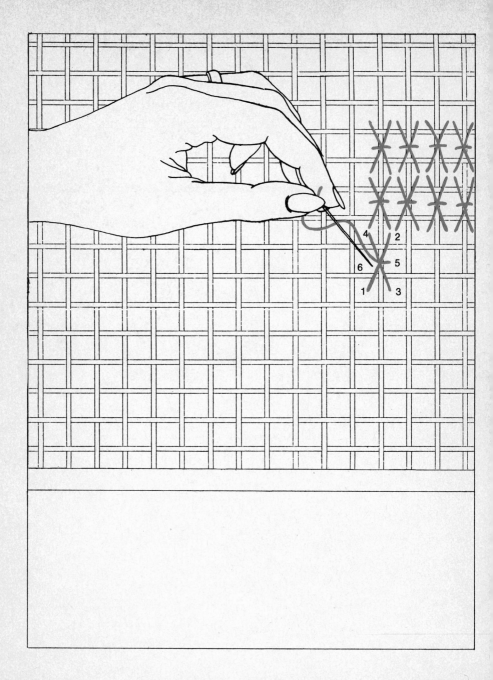

Long Cross Stitch with an Overstitch

The Long Cross Stitch with an Overstitch is still another variation of the basic Cross Stitch. Due to the overstitch it should be worked over three — but no more than five — meshes, as shown in the drawing; the skipped mesh is necessary for the overstitch. If your long stitch is three meshes in length, your overstitch should cover the second mesh; if five meshes long, then your overstitch should cover the third mesh. This divides the stitch evenly above and below the overstitch. The stitch is a sturdy one, will not pull your canvas out of shape, and can be done on either penelope or mono canvas, but it uses more wool than most stitches. It is recommended for border designs; usually two rows of them look just right. Remember to be sure your crosses all go in the same direction.

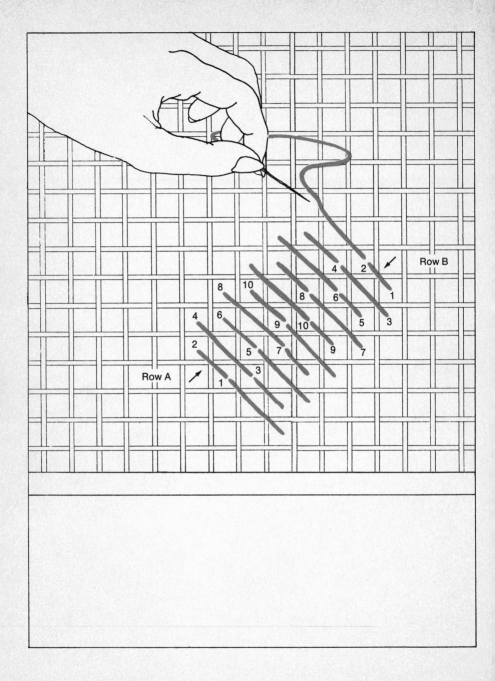

Mosaic Stitch

For the Mosaic Stitch, which is a series of alternating short and long stitches set in a diagonal row, the method of working, illustrated in the drawing, can be the most flexible. Begin your first row (A) across the largest area necessary to work. Then work the next row (B) to fill the shorter areas on either side, continue with alternating rows until the area is filled. It can also be a good time to plan for using an alternating color for each row. The Tent Stitch can be used to cover any open meshes that were not filled by your Mosaic Stitch.

It may help you create a rhythm of stitching if your first row is marked lightly. Then after the first row, you should have no problems. This makes a good border stitch.

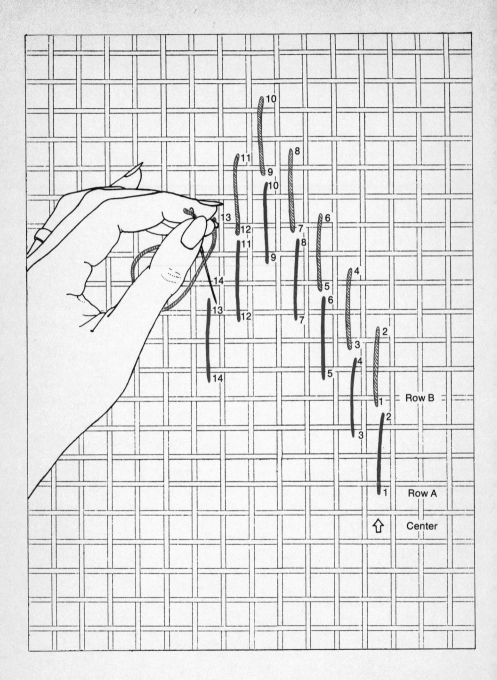

Row B

Row A

Center

36

Bargello Stitch or Flame Stitch

Although it is called a stitch, I have always considered Bargello a design. You can allow your color imagination to run wild with Bargello, which can be worked on any size canvas, and in which your colors can be as many rows deep as you wish. The basic stitch is the Gobelin Stitch, four meshes long.

The pattern I have shown in the following instructions is the basic zigzag design. It is worked on ten-mesh mono canvas with a soft rug yarn. This is a fast-working combination and will give you the satisfaction of seeing your design and color take shape quickly. The stitch is four meshes long and when working up the canvas I planned the extension of the succeeding stitch to cover two mesh threads above the previous stitch. When working the down pattern extend your stitch two meshes below the previous stitch. This series will create a deep peak effect. A shallow effect can be created by grouping two or three successive stitches next to each other and then just covering one mesh beyond as you progress up or down the canvas.

The pillow shown in the photograph was worked in five colors — beginning with a medium blue, continuing with three shades of yellow ranging from mustard yellow to light buff, and finishing in off-white. The repeating of colors begins with medium blue. Any combination of colors can be used as long as they are pleasant when laid alongside each other.

Starting at the bottom of your canvas, count your meshes and then mark the exact center so that your design will be evenly distributed to the left and right. You can also achieve this by folding your canvas in half and marking the center at the bottom and the top. The top marking will indicate the high point of your

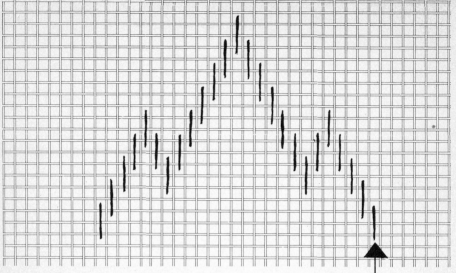

Begin repeat and continue to end of canvas.

38

Bargello pillow worked on 10-mesh mono canvas with soft rug yarn

flame in the final row of your stitching. The bottom mark will indicate the low point of the "flame."

Start your Gobelin Stitch four meshes long. Your next stitch will be one mesh to the left and two meshes up; continue in the same way, completing five stitches. Then, working the same one mesh over but two meshes down, do two stitches down the canvas, after which, repeating the up count, work six stitches up the canvas. Now you repeat the down count, working six stitches down the canvas. Next repeat the two stitches, working up the canvas and again four stitches down the canvas. (Refer to the diagram.) Continue this series as detailed here until you have reached the left end of your canvas, but keep in mind that you will leave 1½ to 2 inches of unworked canvas for finishing your work. Then, starting at your center low point, work in the same manner toward the right, making sure that all of your high points and low points are in line with what you have done on the left side of the canvas. Also, you will have to be careful that the right side of your canvas ends at the same point as the left side of the canvas. The first row is the slowest and will take careful counting to complete but, as you will note in the drawing of the shaded stitch, the rest of the rows will automatically fall into place no matter how many rows of color you have decided you will use in your design.

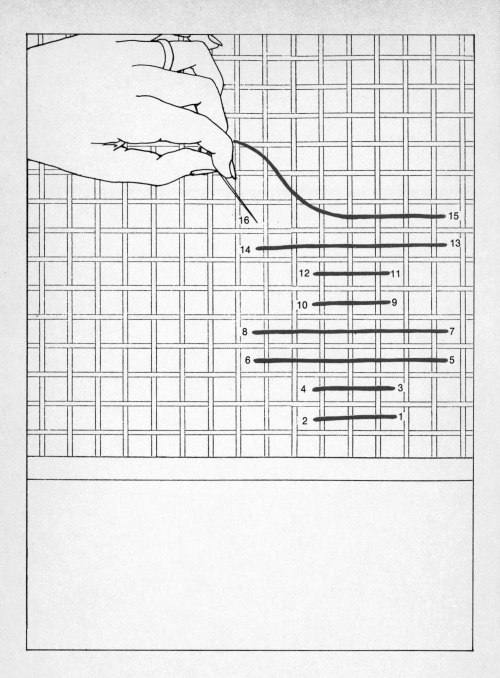

Old Florentine Stitch

The Old Florentine Stitch is part of a series of long-and-short stitch combinations. Your first row may go slowly because you have to count the meshes, but marking your canvas lightly should help. Your long stitch should not be too long, otherwise it can snag; eight meshes is about the right length, if your short stitch is to be four meshes. You can use alternating colors for each stitch length.

For the left-handed needlepointer, working horizontally across the canvas may be the easiest method.

This fast-working stitch, which doesn't use much wool, doesn't have a strong backing.

When you finish your first row, turn your canvas upside down and work the reverse series of stitches so that the long stitch fits into the short stitch and the short stitch fits into the long.

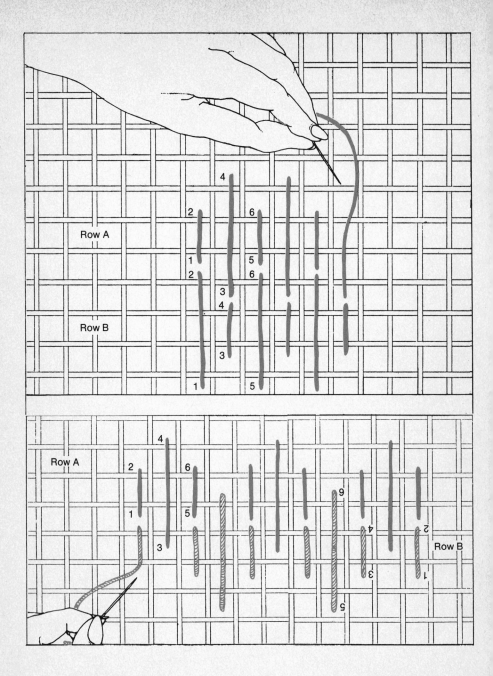

Row A

Row B

Parisian Stitch

The Parisian Stitch and the Hungarian Stitch are somewhat similar, which will be evident if you study the diagrams. The stitch is versatile and can be worked in two colors — alternating the color for each row or alternating the color of your long and short stitch. It is sometimes worked vertically up and down the canvas for a change of design. I recommend that you do this simple alternating short-and-long-stitch, as shown in the drawing, on mono canvas for flexibility in handling your canvas and counting the meshes for your stitches. However, this is not a hard-and-fast rule.

Work Row A until you have finished that line across the canvas. Return to the beginning of your first row and start the next row directly underneath, alternating the length of the stitch that you began with in the previous row.

Hungarian Stitch

The Hungarian Stitch is a perfect filler for the Bargello and is particularly lovely worked in two colors. It bears some resemblance to the Parisian Stitch. Since it is another variation of the Gobelin Stitch, the length of the stitch — three meshes for the short stitch and five meshes for the long stitch — fits the top and bottom of your canvas after you have finished the Bargello design.

You will need to concentrate carefully for the first few rows, but when the rhythm is established, the stitch will work easily. Study the diagram carefully. You will see that all your short stitches line up vertically in a row; the same with your long stitches. When you begin Row A, do the stitches marked 1 through 6, skip a row of meshes, and continue as shown. Begin Row B directly below the last stitch of Row A and continue to the end of that row as shown. If it is necessary to have more than two rows of filler stitches, repeat again the stitches in Row A.

Star Stitch

The Star Stitch forms a lovely design, but since it is slow-working, it is usually reserved for minor detailing. With use of alternating colors, you can make a beautiful border consisting of Star Stitches. The stitch is worked with eight strokes going into a single mesh. Plan your stitch and row carefully so that your canvas will not show.

A single thread of Persian wool easily fits into the popular fourteen-mesh mono canvas; on ten-mesh penelope canvas, use a single thread of Persian wool doubled over.

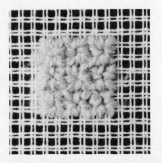

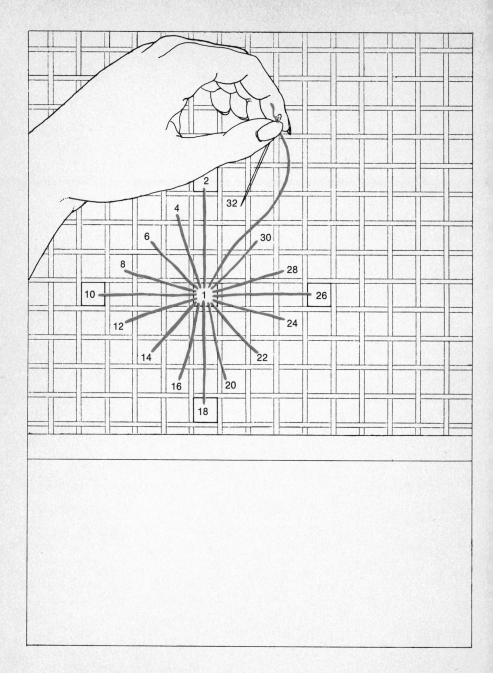

Diamond Stitch

Another lovely stitch, the Diamond Stitch, is only useful for decorative purposes, since it is slow-working and uses so much wool. Sometimes silk thread doubled through the needle will meet the particular requirements of your canvas. A single thread of Persian wool doubled over will fit easily into fourteen-mesh mono canvas. You must be sure your canvas is covered, however, and also that your needle is able to go through the single mesh the required number of times.

Mark the center and the four furthest mesh points of your canvas with a light pencil mark, then proceed as shown in the drawing. Bring your wool from under your canvas at 1, go back into the canvas at 2, and come up from under the canvas again at 1. This procedure is followed for all the strokes 2 through 32.

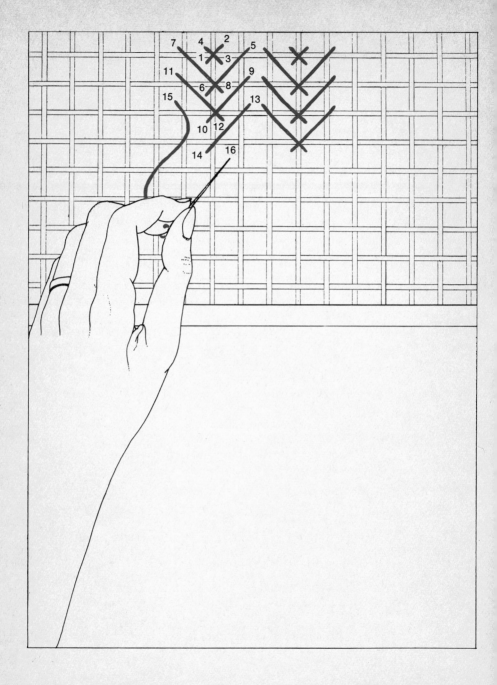

Fern Stitch

The Fern Stitch is an easy, pleasant stitch, which will look fat and fluffy and cover your canvas well with a strong backing. It begins with a Cross Stitch; numbers 1-4 then continue through to steps 15-16 as shown in the drawing. Begin each row at the top of your canvas and work down. The thick braided look of the stitch will give the ribbed effect that a design may call for. The stitch can be used in floral designs for leaves or branches. It is also sometimes used as a filler stitch in small areas of unusual shape.

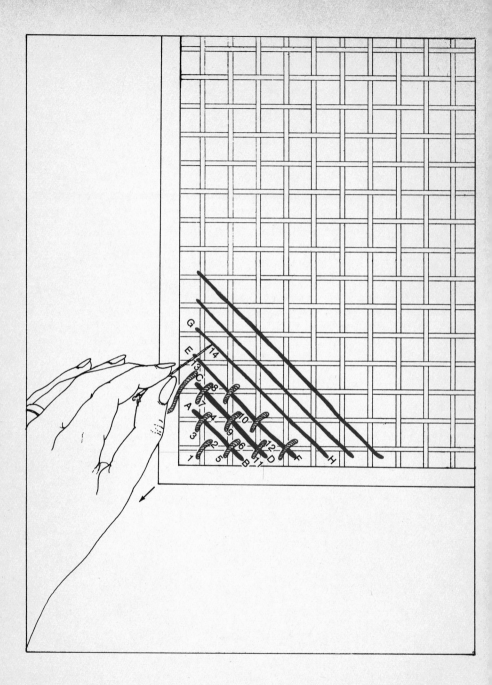

Web Stitch

The Web Stitch is simply a combination of Tramé done diagonally and the Half Cross Stitch, or, to put it another way, a long diagonal stitch secured by small stitches. This stitch is strong and gives you a good backing, but since it uses a great deal of wool and takes time to do, it is recommended for special detailing only. To make it easy on your eyes plan to use it on large mesh canvas only. Notice that the Tramé (solid color and marked by letters A through H) is not woven through the canvas, but simply stitched straight across. The Half Cross Stitch (numbered stitches 1 through 14) then becomes an into-the-canvas-and-up-from-beneath stitch instead of being completed in one operation. Do all your Tramé stitches first, return to your first row and begin all the top stitches. You will notice that the top stitch is worked over every crossing of the vertical and horizontal threads of your canvas.

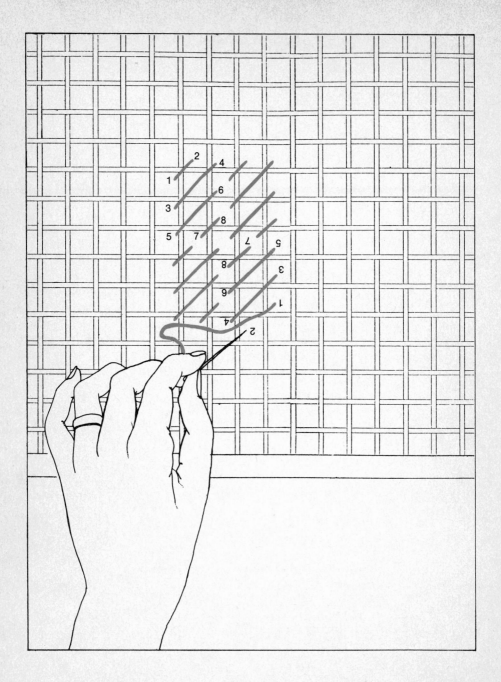

Cashmere Stitch

The Cashmere Stitch is a simple stitch that can be worked either vertically down the canvas or horizontally across the canvas, and with careful marking on your canvas, you can work it in a diagonal pattern. The Cashmere Stitch is a series of one short, two long, and one short stitches. You will notice in the drawing how they all fit to form a square or rectangle, depending on how many of the series you decide to work. However you decide to stitch it, mark your first row lightly, to help you establish your rhythm.

The use of alternating colors will make for an interesting design. You may work four squares in one color and alternate your color for the next four squares. You may also work in alternating rows of color. Begin at the upper left of the space to be filled and turn your canvas upside down for your second row of stitches.

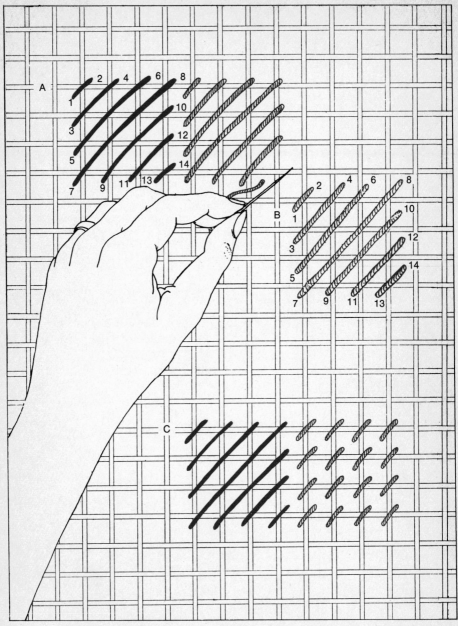

A. *Plaid pattern.* B. *Diagonal.* C. *Checker Stitch.*

Scotch Stitch

The Scotch, a variation of the Mosaic Stitch, is worked over squares of meshes. I recommend four meshes as a good size for your biggest stitch, since it will create a pleasant pattern and your stitches will not be so large that they will snag. The Scotch Stitch can be worked in any number of designs, either using different colors as shown in the drawing A, or combined with another stitch that creates a checkered pattern, as in Drawing C, in which the Scotch Stitch is combined with the simple Half Cross Stitch. A handsome pattern can be created by stitching half of your square numbers (1-6) in one color and the other half (7-14) in a contrasting color. Another variation is to change the directions your stitch will go with each square and finally do step 7-8 in another color. A diagonal pattern of color can be created by repeating the stitch series. Skip a mesh and begin with No. 1 again as shown in the shaded stitches in B.

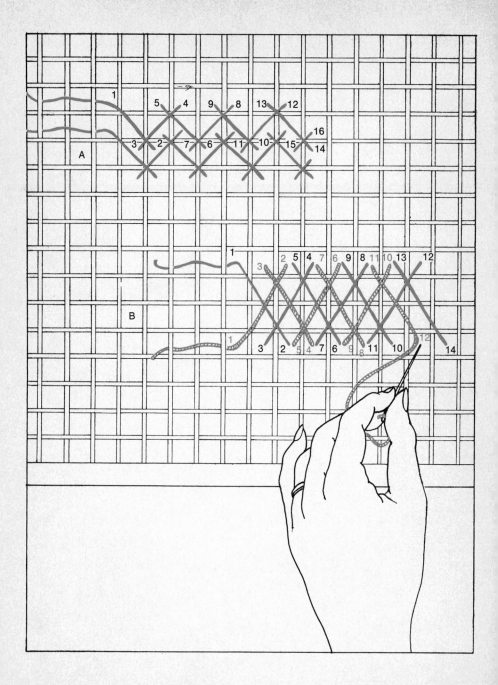

Herringbone Stitch

Single Color Herringbone that may also be used with shades of one color

Two-Color Herringbone

Finally, a stitch made just for the left-handed! The Herringbone Stitch can only be worked from the left to the right. You must end your wool at the final stitch of each row and begin anew at the left again. If possible, weave your wool in and out of the canvas beyond your stitch range (see the drawing), since the usual beginning and ending of the rows will create unnecessary bulk at these two points of your canvas. Sometimes the stitch is recommended only for penelope canvas as the backing is not very firm; however, it can be used on mono canvas too if you make sure to pull the stitches firm. I have found that the stitch will work faster and with less eye strain if I use it on large-mesh canvas. Therefore, it is an ideal stitch for rug canvas in which it creates a tweedy effect. Do not use the Herringbone Stitch as a filler stitch, again because the backing is not strong enough.

When working with the single-color Herringbone Stitch, each row is completed as you work across the canvas. Return to the left side of your canvas and begin the next row. This stitch is lovely when worked in a pattern of varied colors, such as shades of gray for each row that begin with a row of white and finish with a row of deep charcoal gray or black. Repeat all the colors again from the row of white on.

You will notice in the drawing that the Herringbone Stitch done with two colors is slightly different from the stitch done in one color; both the width and length of the meshes covered are greater. The understitch (in solid color with black numbers) is worked first. Then your second color (shaded lines and colored numbers) is worked over the first stitch. You might find it easier to mark your canvas lightly for color identification of stitches.

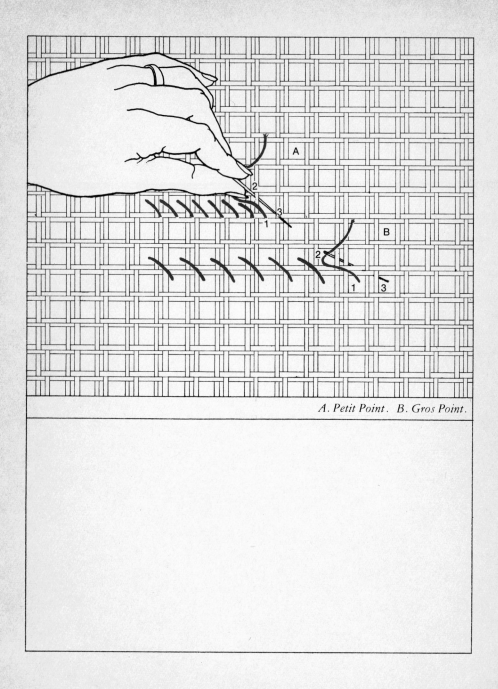

A. Petit Point. B. Gros Point.

Petit Point
Combined with Gros Point

Petit Point is actually the simple Continental Stitch worked over every thread of the penelope canvas instead of the double thread. It is most effective when combined with Gros Point, which is the Continental Stitch over the double threads of the canvas. These two stitches complement each other and give you a flexibility in designing your canvas and in selecting the materials you will use.

The Petit Point design may be worked in silk and you will thus achieve some beautiful highlights. A less expensive method is to use a single thread of a three-thread strand of Persian wool; use the full strand for your Gros Point. Crewel made of fine twisted wool is also often used for Petit Point. Experiment on a piece of canvas until you get the effect that appeals to your eye, keeping in mind that your wool or silk must be the proper weight to cover your canvas threads. Use short lengths of wool when working your Petit Point, since constant pulling through the tiny mesh openings would give your wool a "pulled" look.

Designing Your Own Needlepoint Canvas

The first thing to be sure of is that you have a definite idea how your finished work will be used. This will help you decide on the size of the canvas and, most important, what your design will be. Your ideas about what your design should be will come from whatever is around you. Your design may be inspired by your family or your desire to record something very personal pertaining to them, or another hobby. Anything that is part of your world may give you the idea.

The nice thing about canvas work is that, if you like, there is no reason to be realistic, or else you can copy and trace anything that appeals to you. Above all, the most important thing to keep in mind when planning your first attempts is to keep them simple. Lettering or some of today's modern paintings can be a great source of design ideas. Use brilliant colors, because what may look wild in the skein will be just right on the canvas. If you want a figure to really stand out, use a black outline; or if you have a dark object on a dark background, surround the object with an outline whose color is a lighter version than the object's color.

If your design calls for a combination of simple needlepoint background and fine detail petit point, you must use a penelope canvas. This means that you will separate the warp and woof threads to simulate a mono canvas for the petit point. For instance, a nine-mesh-to-the-inch penelope canvas will separate

to an eighteen-mesh mono canvas for the detailing. However, for this more complex work, I believe that you should wait until you are more confident in handling your own designs.

For almost twenty years I have been especially exposed to typography, and so for one of my personal designs, I just turned to words and letters, which can easily be blocked out on graph squares.

The simplest method of working out a design is by using graph paper. Each square counts as a stitch. Of course, it is most convenient to have your graph squares per inch equal your canvas squares, but this is not always possible. For instance, graph paper is not available in fourteen squares to the inch, which is a popular size in mono canvas. So, using the paper that comes closest in squares to your canvas, begin by finding the exact center of the paper and mark it with a pencil dot. Then working out from the center, start to sketch your design. This is the time for all the erasing and redoing of your drawing. When you are satisfied with your thoughts on paper — making sure that you have worked out from the center in such a way that the design is laid out evenly in all four directions, and that the spacing between each similar part of your design is equal — use a firm pencil and begin to block in the design. There is still time for any corrections. The final step on the graph paper is to fill your design in with the colors you plan to use. Start by using pieces of colored paper until you find the combination that appeals to you. Then color directly on the design, keeping in mind that wools are manufactured in such a great variety of colors that you might want to brighten or deepen the color when you come to the point of actual purchase.

When all is as you wish it to be, take a deep breath!! You are ready.

Begin your transfer to the canvas by marking the center with a lightly inked square. For this use a laundry marking pen, since it is waterproof and dry-cleaning proof. Also mark the outer boundaries of your work after carefully counting the meshes in all four directions, but don't forget to leave a two-inch border of unworked canvas for finishing. If your canvas is the same square-

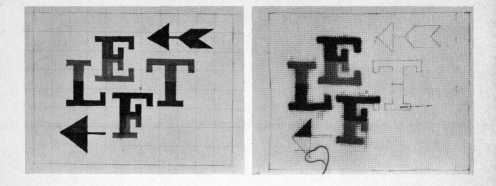

to-the-inch size as your graph paper, use dressmaker carbon and a sharp pencil and trace your design directly onto the canvas. Dressmaker carbon comes in several different colors and will not smudge. If you wish to darken the lines, go over the tracing with the laundry marking pen. Most times, however, your graph size will not match your canvas size. In these cases, start at the center marking on the graph, counting and marking the corresponding number of squares on your canvas until you have completed the design. Don't be concerned that your graph square is not the same as your canvas mesh size. What matters is the number of meshes that you have counted out.

For the simplest color guide, I have found it useful to mark my canvas lightly with the laundry marker, putting down the first initial of the color, and I also refer back to my graph work sheet. So many paints take time to dry or are not absolutely waterproof, in addition to being an unnecessary expense, that painting the canvas doesn't seem as practical.

Occasionally the design you wish to use for your canvas is the same size as your canvas, or can be photostated to the size you will need for your canvas. The easiest way of transferring is then to use the "sunny window" method. Tape your original design to a window pane, preferably a sunny exposure, then tape your canvas directly over it. Make sure the design is centered in your canvas; use the laundry marker and mark the center and four

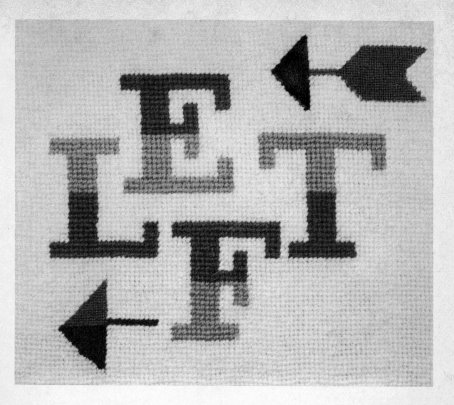

corners of your design and continue to trace the design onto the canvas.

When your needlework is completed, the next step of your work is to block the canvas back into shape. No matter how you have tried not to pull your stitches too tight or what stitches you have worked, there will be some distortion. Use a sewing machine, if available, and stitch two rows of machine stitching on your unworked canvas. Stitch the first row about a half inch from your finished needlework, and the second a half inch beyond the first row. This will prevent your canvas from raveling. Cut off the excess canvas beyond the second row of stitches.

While working my needlepoint, I frequently spray the work with Scotch-gard to keep it from becoming too soiled. Therefore, the next step is done only if necessary, to clean your needlework. Dip the canvas in cold water that has a bit of Woolite added to it. Roll the canvas into a towel to remove any excess water;

however, do not allow it to remain rolled in the towel for too long a time. Use a board (I use an old pastry board) and begin to gently stretch and pull your damp canvas into shape, tacking it down to the board as you are pulling. Place your tacks close together to keep the canvas firmly in place. Allow the canvas to remain this way until it is thoroughly dry. If your needlework has not become too soiled while you have been stitching, block it with a steam iron and a damp cloth, pulling it hard against the direction of the distortion. Pin it to your ironing board cover and press it dry.

If your finished needlework is to be a wall hanging, it may be blocked into shape by tacking it to a canvas stretcher while it is damp and when it is thoroughly dry, hang it with picture wire. Canvas stretchers are available in art supply or picture frame shops.

To use your needlework as a pillow covering, sew your finished canvas to a piece of fabric, preferably lightweight upholstery fabric that matches the predominant color in your canvas. Place both the canvas and material together with the insides out, pin, and machine stitch. Sew with the canvas on the top so that you can be sure that your machine sewing will come between the finished work and the next vertical canvas thread. In this way you will see to it that no part of your unworked canvas will show on the outside of the finished pillow. Sew two rows of machine stitching for added strength. Sew three sides of your cover, turn the cover to its right side, and press lightly for a knife edge to your seams. Insert your pillow and turn in the edges of the fourth side, pin, and finish by sewing by hand, using a slip stitch.

I suggest that rugs, handbags, and some of the other accessories should be handled by professional finishers.